Infatuation

Poems of the Heart
by Alexandra H. Rodrigues

ACKNOWLEDGMENTS

In appreciation to my critic Thaddeus Hutyra for his help and encouragement. This book could not have been published without the persistence of my editor and designer Gloria Savini Kraemer. My thank you goes out to Janet Pomeranz for her honest and thoughtful critiques. Also, I take this opportunity to thank Mary Haughey, my writing instructor at the local library for, the confidence to publish she instills in her students.

The author has been frequently published in
Great South Bay Magazine,
The Creativity Webzine, Cocktailmolly, Postcard Shorts,
Eber & Wein, South Bay's Neighbor,
Famous Poets of the Heartland, and
Pan Am Historical Foundation.

Love or Lust

If all it is, is lust
It is over after the last thrust.
If it is only love
It can last but can get rough.
If it is love and lust
You have reason the future to trust.

If you settle for only lust
Infatuation could become disgust.
If you settle for only love
Chance is that the nights will get tough.
If love and lust are in the cards
You'll come to reap deserved rewards.

Be You

We talk and we talk and what do we say
"How are you" or "Have a good day."
Nothing but truly hollow words
is what in that case to me occurs.

For politics or small talk that holds true
same as for relationships or what is new.
Most of the information we are usually fed
changes its core every minute I bet.

Communication has become a game.
So much value is lost, it is a shame.
In old times a few honest words were enough
to conquer a lifestyle that was quite rough.

"Love" already when spoken might be obsolete.
Was only uttered to absorb a need.
A whole stream of empty, useless words
is often so dumb it nearly hurts.

Only in poetry hidden messages should be allowed
but society wants with words to hypnotize the crowd.
Our demeanor can more often relay the truth
We would be better if gestures we choose.

Touch, hug, expose yourself and your thought,
feel free to let yourself in actions be caught.
No empty words, just be true,
I need to know who is really you!

A Strange Hurt

To lose a lover is sad and it hurts
More so when pride and grief mingle in spurts.
The smartest route for the future would be
To avoid any occasion where your face I see.

Worse it would even be if you were with her
As that would, what we had, again to the surface stir.
What furthermore does rip my inners apart,
Is, when with writes you open to her your heart.

All that which for myself to reach I had hoped
Now into another love of yours has eloped.
The pain in my heart and soul is so severe
From my horizon I will try to make you disappear.

Away from you, I'll force any emotion to turn to stone.
Stripped of hope I will vegetate all alone.
To return to my old ways, I will try, if I must.
To the times when I had no interest in love or in lust.

I will return to the existence when I was adrift
To the time before I met you and you gave me a lift.
You filled a short period with exhilarating bliss.
Something when turned to stone, I will not miss.

At this moment in time I still grind my teeth
Planning and scheming to affect my release.

Longing

To ask for the truth, I am afraid.
What I do not want to hear
may be said.
My mind and my body love you.
A sensation that surprises me
daily anew.

I want to be with you in
body and mind.
Hope that in me an unknown
thrill you will find.
Call out my name in ecstasy.
The perfect lover you would be.

I felt your touch in dreams
night after night.
Nothing you could do wrong.
Every kiss, every movement
that you gave me
was placed just right.

To experience this in reality
Our climax in accord
Could arouse our sex and embrace
by merging our individuality,
with lust and love into a gift
From an alien space.

Waiting

I fell in love
I can't get up
Till you come and give me a hand.

Since I know of you
My blatant disregard of my
Bodily needs just went.

When I think of you
Needles of lust consume me
Together in mind and body
With you I want to be.

The aura of a totally new life
Embraces all for what I strive.
You are on my mind.

You are in my mind
In my imagination, in all that is me.
What I used to think was love
Now turns out to have been bluff.

My vibes that swing in the Universe
All carry the image you intonate
It is for you I desperately wait.

Hello Angel

How should I picture myself
When in the unknown sphere I delve?
How should I picture you and you and you
Who knows the image that is true?

Sometimes the very belief
That we need to be complete
Turns understanding into grief.

Our bodies we know are nothing but shell
Where is the soul we are guarding from hell?
Soul – "he is a good soul" – we sometimes hear
Without soul all that is left is fear.

Once lost, faith is hard to retrieve
It needs to be done before earth you leave
What is the reason for which millions have lived?
Is death itself the ultimate gift?

The divine purpose rests behind star after star
Reincarnation aloof and soo far.
We are not chosen to know what the answer is
We can only hope for the ultimate bliss.

Either Or

You drive me nuts when you put me under your spell
Unable to feel your touch equals burning in hell.
Any description of either true or of want to be
One can in the universe of poets see.

I realize how very cautious you are in this play
The minute it becomes personal you end your stay.
Ruthlessly the unison that only in my dreams is true
Kindles the fire in my veins each day anew.

There has to be a mythical connection
The cause and source of it still awaits detection.
Spiritual forces unknown to me or you
Into this endeavor of alien love me threw.

Reality has always held me in an iron grip.
Yet now I am willing into dreamland to slip.
Oddly at this point your presence has becomes so real
With unknown pleasures I'm granted to deal.

Our thoughts are the managers of our life
Like in a car we control the drive.
It's up to us not out of shape to bend
To select the sphere in which our time to spend.

Go With the Flow

A stabbing feeling of unsatisfied lust
A nagging urge causes my pride disgust
Where and when did this originate?
Is it love or need for an escapade?

Is it nothing more than a chemical reaction?
Resulting from a recent in-depth attraction?
Does it in my chosen one reverberate?
Will he be able to my want to relate?

Will the thrill survive the act?
May it be is wiser not to challenge the fact?
Dreams often surpass in quality
Any ultimately finalized reality.

How it happens I really do not know,
For better or worse I will go with the flow.

I Want You!

I want you to know
That I love you so
It fills me with surrealistic glow
Electric sparks of joy I could throw

It appears a miracle happened yesterday
It will hurt if you do not also see it that way
A lot out of the depth of our souls let's share
Reality of itself will take care

Let us imagine how it all could be
To play and to hope one is always free
In exchanging what stimulates our drive
We might at an intimate relation of thoughts arrive

We could to this charade as love in Technicolor refer
Please do play! Do not my fun deter!

"And that is so."

It is said
The eyes we should call
The mirror of the soul.
　And that is so.

Never will be my friend
Whose demeanor denies
That I look deep into his eyes.
　And that is so.

The lowering,
And the blinking of someone's eyes
In my mind a secret hides.
　And that is so.

Yet, I have never been able
Into Your, my lover's eyes, to see.
Our hearts are said to hold the key.
　And that is so.

Onto the firmament
In his mercy God put there
Four stars, for each of us a pair.
  And that is so.

They present eyes
That lock in unison and shine.
Like the Big Dipper a heavenly sign.
  And that is so.

Although bodily far apart
When we look at the sky
We suddenly see eye to eye
  And that is so.

A divine power
Helped your and my soul
That our juices together flow
  And that is so.

Avoid

How did it happen?
Why was I so blind?
Your spell, your fine words
Had hypnotized my mind.

I did not mind pleading
Wanted that you love me too
Whatever you said
I believed to be true.

Then I saw you together
She acted mesmerized by you
I heard you say many an endearing word
Those I knew, and that really hurt.

The same body language
That with me you had used
With lingering anguish
I now saw you into her infuse.

More than losing the love
 I had hoped for so much
Stung that you made a fool out of me
While I yearned for your touch.

You deceived many others
As time went by!
In disbelief I shake my head
My past ignorance makes me sigh.

To these loopholes into which we fall
Which then for months or years us gall
We need to pay close attention
To avoid repetition of what I did mention.

Just One

One Kiss
Just one kiss from you
would mean more than any kiss
I ever got.

One Rose
Just one rose from you would stay
with me dried, pressed and
safe-guarded for life.

One Rainbow
Just one rainbow would watch
us holding hands and promising
us to each other.

One Day
Just one day it might happen
that the "would" could turn
into "so be it."

Darling

Hello my darling, surprised I am using this noun?
Forgive me, it seems that in confusion I drown.
"Darling" is a word that never before in muse
I have elected as endearment to choose.

Sweetheart, lover, angel, friend
Were the words I mostly had at hand.
It is that I want something special for you,
As you make me feel what to me is new.

If in vulgar, erotic style I would dare to write
We both might easily experience delight.
Although as I now use the romantic path
Possibilities glitter in gold, silver and brass.

Gold, the moon who has seen our desires,
Silver, the surface of a wind-still lake.
Brass, the sound of a final crescendo
Which into higher spheres us will take.

I am getting more skilled in telepathy
Which I use when I feel the urge with you to be.
I then picture us together in total elation
Totally engulfed by delicious temptation

My darling with this I will end for today
Before too many uncalled for things I say.
Together let's reach a thrilling pleasure
Imagination being the blessed treasure.

Freedom of Night

The magic of my dreamland was torn.
It stayed with the night.
I had awoken to a day remorsefully bright.
The dream of you and me is gone,
Lingering in my mind but shying the sun.

In my night visions there is no inhibition.
Irks and quirks underlie no condition.
My soul and body are an open book
Into which in real life no one may look.

I experience thrills and vibes coming from you.
They make my dream feel oh so true.
Together a total merge we undergo
The elixir to have ecstasy does grow.

Daily life rejects our deep desire.
Too many rules earthly love does require.
Pride curtails even our very own pleasure
As we apply the sociable acceptable measure.

I close my eyes and hope night comes soon again
When in my dreams you are my biggest fan.
When of all restrictions I am free
When my own self I am allowed to be.

Family Nevertheless

They had agreed with each other to meet.
Quickly a place they found for their need.
Chosen was a luscious, green hedge,
with pink garlands of roses along the edge.
A brown bench, painted and made out of wood
Surely would their mediations nicely suit.
It was sturdy and inviting for two.
Certainly for one of the nymphs it would do.

A path sprinkled with shells led to the river
Into which waterfalls their drops let quiver.
It marked an aura of constant activity
No question for which nymph this spot would be.
The nymph called Love all dressed in white lace
had decided that under the rose bush was her place.
Here her enrichment could happily grow.
In nurturing blossoms she was a pro.

Nymph Trust wore blue and a veil with jewel tips.
She sat on the brown bench, a smile on her lips.
The third nymph, named Lust, did fidget around.
To patience she never ever felt bound.
Her slinky body in a tight dress, red and gold
exposed a sumptuous, naked body in every fold.

They rarely felt the need with each other to bother.
By themselves neither of them felt truly safe.
One, for one of the other would mostly crave.
He often was called to settle their disputes.
Kindness always stayed calm, never was rude.
We humans are welcome their powers to use.
Sadly quite often, one or two we would abuse.
Today in a fluke of open-mindedness,
They had invited their relative, named Kindness.
The three looked doubtfully at each other.

They saw him, knew that fun it was going to be!
Today Trust, Love, Lust and Kindness will be family.
If only in our human, often confusing environment,
with all four of them together our time could be spent!

I Need to Believe

Let me trust in what I want to believe.
Let my emotions be protected from grief.
Let me believe that it is true what I've seen.
Let me ignore what it really has been.

With words that you sent in a song my way,
I make believe you wanted to me them relay.
Even if you did not really mean them for me,
I do them as answers to my questions see.

After such fabricated happiness
The truth hits like an ice-cold kiss.
I wonder if you even understand,
That my mental costume is in your hand.

Yet there is a thrilling sensation in this tease
Despite that my soul splinters piece by piece.
Common sense warrants to stop it all.
It is so obvious that I am going to fall.

Let me trust in what I want to believe.
Let my emotions be protected from grief.
Let me not ever come, what is, to regret.
Let me keep the trust that our souls have met.

Hit or Miss

A Hate-Love relationship it is.
Each day challenged by a hit or miss.
Yesterday I stayed with him
In each other's passion we did swim.

Came morning I left him without a word.
Now it's evening again, from him I have not heard.
Does somebody else please him in the night?
Who will satisfy him to an explosive delight?

No call from him on day two or three.
By now I was giddy, him I wanted to see.
Nearly losing my mind by day four.
Finally there was a knock at the door.

"Why did you without notice take your leave?
Snuck out and never called just like a thief?
Forgive me, I had to learn the hard way.
Despite all your escapades I know I must stay."

A lesson I had wanted to teach this man
That a woman also promiscuously acting can.
But the tables were turned on me.
Being loved can be lost by being too free.

For a Split Second

Where have I been?
The World I have seen!
Still only the surface I did touch.
Feelings never amounted to much.

Lately I experience thrill after thrill,
Seemingly obsessed despite my will,
Steered by an alien and tantalizing force,
With you being the leader of course.

Despite that once I was hungry for sex
Your spell seems to be of a different hex.
As you bodily fulfilled me once by chance
A deeper want now causes a trance.

If ever I could the two combine,
Any desire on its own would resign.
A total ecstasy would be my fate
Like air bubbles through you I would dissipate.

I gladly settle for a small moment in time
Wishing to be allowed to say "You are mine."

Tell Me

Every fiber in my body yearns for you
Not for the You I know
But for the one I wish I knew.

That you are kind and smart is
Clear to me
Yet your inner self I ache to see.

When words at times are really deep
You tend your reaction
From me hidden to keep.

All I ask is that you make no excuse
If you feel it is over
Just tell me the truth.

Even if I will be deeply hurt inside
With time I will be able
To swallow my pride.

Just give me a reason,
Give me a "Why"
I want to know you, do not deny!

What Now?

I am torn between admiring and cursing you.
My spirits skim between a high and a blue.
I cannot even tell of what you are aware!
Did you ever consider your soul to share?

You send romantic, amazing poems my way.
Then negate all that in conversation you say.
Whatever is happening I can never be sure.
This uncertainty warrants some kind of cure.

Whatever is happening I made it all up.
One word of real love would be like winning the Davis Cup.
Many times I feel ridiculous.
I am not a stalker, no not this!

Yet what has happened to my pride
Even in all my illusions it does not feel right.
Imagination, illusion, love, hate, a frightening mix.
It's a wonder I do not grab a quick fix.

Because I don't know how you really feel
I need to be cautious at what for now is the deal.
Hopefully my body gives me permission
To stop and quit all this for a sound decision.

Although I understand that the illusion is self-made
For a short time of a difference in my life I would trade.
Everything but my self-worth I would gamble away
But I have no power over what will happen next day.
 Not being in charge of destiny and time
 I will make believe that you are mine.

Corynn

There is more life in a skull than in her face
There was no emotion after their embrace
She appeared to have turned into stone
No elation, no joy not even disgust or hone
He did read it clearly in her eyes
Her feeling had suddenly said its goodbyes.

What had happened, what had he done?
On her own she had willingly to him come
Without any question they had had good fun.
Yet at this minute she looked like she wanted to run.
He asked, "My dear why do you look as if I committed a sin?"
She whispered, "My name is Elvira – you called me Corynn."

Bouncing Around

How can I travel on an even road?
How can I my mood swings decode?
From complete and perfect satisfaction
to a confusing, aching imperfection.

Up – Up	Utter Elation
Down – Down	Devastation
Right – Right	Rhythm of Tango delight
Left – Left	Leaves my heart cast aside
High	Hearing what the stars us tell
Low	Leading surely to life in hell.

How can I find answer to what is on my mind?
"Where and how can I harmony find?"

Destiny Joke

There are words that weigh heavy on my chest
"I love you" "I want you" "You are the best"
Forbidden to speak them they get harder to carry
Day to day, you the one they are meant for,
Hesitates to open the dividing door.

On the other hand there is another man I know
Who suffers with these words; in his heart they grow
He would like me to be quite a bit more receptive
But realizes , this is not for what I now live.

Is it that we all want mostly what we can't get?
It is a maze of emotions among world's lovers set
Experience in life shows us often enough
That after reaching a goal the going gets rough.

It is the wanting that causes the enticing thrill
Once satisfied often all urge turns to nil.
Notice, I really have been through it all
But again and again under the spell of
"I want him" I fall.

Now What?

Independence and ignorance are hard to bear
Often I sense that into a vacuum I stare.
To be constantly bounced from hope to despair
Is extremely frustrating and not quite fair.

I want nothing that you are not willing to give.
For many years I did with mediocrity live.
That was, when it was me, who played with make believe
Me, who owes my partner apologies for that grief.

May be I am absolved because that man never knew
That I was a master in making evasions sound true
On the other hand I am very sensitive and detect the truth.
For lies, no matter how flattering, I have no use.

Presently I myself am steadily deceiving my mind
To the word – impossible – I am purposely blind.
Not sure where to turn or how to act
I issue myself ultimatum after ultimatum to face the fact.

Play With Me

Mind over matter
Is that really better?
I know without the faintest doubt
That what I wish for is for naught.

Still I make myself dream of thee
Imagine the lust if you were with me.
My want is that you be my playmate
And we find a fantasy to relate.

Both of us aware that none of it is true
Each of us will form a phantom after our own view.
In play delightful sensations one can achieve
It will never wounds nor mistrust leave.

I want it to be a game without win or lose
Let's our own fulfillment choose.
These words I tried to carefully mince
I hope they have the power to convince.

Uninvited

Uninvited, out of the blue
The feeling of utter sadness grew.
One cannot always control the body's task
As the face turns into a weird, smudged mask.

The make-up cakes, the lipstick smears,
Caused by an involuntary burst of tears.
Let the emotions flow, it releases the stress,
Then quickly with fresh powder repair the mess.

Nobody was around to see the true you.
Not even you are given for the reason the clue.
If only a heartache that weighs on your chest
With a dab of make-up could be put to rest!

Secret Thought

My satiny hands touch your most sensitive skin,
Causing a thrill to explode from within.
If this occurs without a deep connection,
It could only be frowned upon as vulgar action.
Yet when intimacy blends into a shared thought,
it will get both of us in the Supernatural caught.

Please Stay

A shadow has fallen over my day,
Without you I feel listless and sad.
Alone, I immediately lost my way.

My heart I had in a solid shell
Till the day that you came
And you put me under your spell.

During no relationship in the past
Did just the thought of the act of love
Such a sensuous picture cast.

With you my best friend and lover
There is the promise of bliss
In the Garden of Eden from cover to cover.

True Love

Love and caring is a sweet mix.
Many mood ailments it can fix.
Look for it when you are in emotional pain.
From the "catch me if you can" play do refrain.

True love does not pursue the "who is better" spiel.
Its power is how it makes you feel.
"For better or for worse"
To retain love one should often rehearse.

Prone

While my mind today is full of you
I prefer to be alone
With all the gentle things you do
You softened my heart of stone.

Many times I have been hurt
And I caused harm just the same
Often it was just a single word
Which for a break-up was to blame.

What seems to be the deepest love
Can come so easily to a halt
It gets to be exposed as bluff
Indifferent it is who is at fault.

When everlasting love we swear
How come we always do forget
Now that we vision us as pair
That before by others our desire was met.

The human mind is meant to think
So maybe we are better off alone
If it were not that so often in a blink
To the desire of the flesh we fall prone.

So Be It

Yes, you will be my downfall and my destiny
From my own thoughts I wish to flee
The urge to experience your touch
Fills my waking hours for sure too much.

To feel so needy puts me to shame
What began so innocently is no longer a game
Nightly erotic images of you and me
In my dreams and during REM cycles I see.

You successfully make turmoil out of my daily life
Forgotten is the hurt of a widowed wife
You tempt me to stamp my feet on the floor
I want so much more, so much more.

I singled you out, with you I excel
Through the written word and signs of love as well
Love? Lust? Call it what you will
Relax, enjoy whatever gives you a thrill.

There are times I want to hide from myself
Turn into a bisque figure on a shelf.
I cannot stop the sensations you ignite
They have proven to give me too much delight.

Who Are You?

Who are you my friend?
By what power were you sent?
Are you here to tempt me?
Wake the devil I can be?

Or is in this a hidden vibe
Hieroglyphs in a godly guide?
If so make sure you will not miss
That it would be special bliss.

You come and you go
Over the when and where I have no control
I listen to my inner voice
There I am told I have no choice.

So surprise me, make my secret inner rise
If it works it will warrant any price.
Good or bad
Sane or mad
Shattering my bones it must be
So that a difference of it all I see.

Your Choice

So why not live in a world of make believe
Where one can refuse to worry or to grieve.
To being showered with the gift of love
Or change in my mind when things get tough.

Why see matters the way they really are?
Why can one not call it near, when it is far?
Why not, when it hurts to be alone
Invite make-believe persons into your home?

Possibly where most of us go wrong
Is that we procrastinate in doubt too long.
We lament and in our woes then get stuck.
Why refuse to attempt to change our luck?

It is up to us and us alone
Which key to play to find the right tone.
If you feel sorry about what is happening to you
The universe is forced to consider it true.

It will be registered in the big black book
As destiny refuses to let it off the hook.
If on the other hand the dilemma we ignore,
Destiny gets the hint that the connection we tore.

The trick is to be convinced that all is well.
That will make the devil choke in hell.
Get rid of whatever is burdening you,
Experience the world as being perfect and true.

Unseen

I don't know how your voice sounds when you speak
I don't know how in the love act elation you seek
I don't know exactly what shade are your eyes
I don't know when your poems tell truth or white lies.

All that is really not pertinent information
As we hardly will ever meet in this equation
It is after our bodies turn into ephemeral souls
That we will hook up with each other like magnetic poles.

You don't know if my skin is silken and smooth
You don't know if I ever get high on booze
You don't know if my moans are high or low
You don't know if my arousal comes fast or slow.

Time will come when our souls attract
Opposite poles in explosion connect
Two units connected by their sensitive points
Will find themselves forever joined.

Pretend to Pretend

My entire life I knew well how to pretend.
My days and yes, even my nights, as a pseudo-me I spent.
I was a Jack of many trades.
Participated in shaping all different fates.

I could change my views like a chameleon.
Not sure where all those talents originated from.
I always admitted to be an actress on the stage of life.
Took advantage of what fitted my narcissistic drive.

Then when you entered my personal sphere,
And I knew that as lover I could not have you dear,
I hoped that Fortuna would teach me humility
At this time when I needed to accept hard reality.

That spark between two people that sets them on fire,
Has with gripping pain become my biggest desire.
With remorse I have become aware that despite the fun,
By pretending and acting a tight net of loneliness I spun.

Till Death Do Us Part

It will – It has!

It does not stop
For beauty
For prosperity
For love or for hate!

So why should we stop
For lost beauty
For lost prosperity
For lost love or for hate?

Why of telling the truth be afraid?
Why of doing as we please be afraid?
Why of showing our true colors be afraid?
And on and on, why be afraid?

What does it mean
– be good
– be brave
– be considerate
And on and on, what does it mean?

Can love conquer the border between now
And then?
Is there an eternity for women and men?

For sure after death we no longer multiply
There will always be the Why? Why? Why?
In this life for sure and maybe in a next one too
The question remains, "What in the world? What in hell?
What, oh God is true?"

Merge

As hazy dew over the mountains does appear,
It evokes in me a sensation of deep-set fear.
I'm not ready yet to watch earth from above,
With only my soul whispering to you my love.

Therefore I hang on every word from you.
I wish that the depth of my infatuation you knew.
Frantically I hold on to our present relation
What we now have is my sole consolation

One day, high above the mountain's pole
What we shared will accompany my soul.
Thus to have our minds and bodies merge,
Remains for now my imminent, unsettling urge

Your Spell

You let me taste the power of your mind.
You teased me till I fell for you blind.
Then suddenly I was to find out
What this was really all about.

To yourself and the world you wanted to prove
That you could direct my every move.
Now that this task you did fulfill,
And like a marionette I obey your will

The thrill is gone for you.
None of your endearments were ever true.
Here now is what is really bad
I am quite furious and very mad.

Your spell was and still is so strong
That despite that I know it to be wrong
I still yearn to cross your way
Anew and anew on every day.

It was you who molded me into this state,
You are responsible for what is my fate.
Smart like you are I hope you come up with a cure
That will make me want to leave you for sure.

My and your well-being are in your hand
Please in the future do not pretend.

Eyes Locked

When will be the day that you open up to me?
When without reservation will your true you I see.
Our kidding and teasing has taken its course
Now truth is knocking with undeniable force.

As of lately I feel a slight melt of your reserve.
Still see no straight path, just curve after curve.
On a road that can only be tiptoed upon
With you I want to venture, with you alone!

Am I hypnotized or just plain in love
The correct answer is often so very tough.
When your eyes lock with mine
I experience knowledge of what is divine.

To the deepest point of the sea
And the highest sphere that can be
My heart and soul races
It wants with you to explore those spaces.

This sensation is so hard to explain
It is overpowering, bordering nearly on pain.
My bodily fibers dance in a joyous swing
While nerves lust and of togetherness sing.

It is those moments I cherish in awe
When in your eyes the urge I saw..

Without Guilt

Yesterday I was ready to exit my fairy tales

Then this morning I still rose to follow

My plan

But then

Some lingering force did not let me go

Your picture popped up

Still we

As close as can be

So I will have to take it step by step

Gently free myself from you

Welcome the delay

Guiltless savor today!

Only You

Take my hands and lead me
Never let me be
You, the phantom of my imagination
You the only one to cause my elation.

When I am together with you
No longer counts what before I knew
An alien thrill spreads over me
You, You and only You I see.

You make what once was truly dark
With hue like glittering diamonds spark
Every fiber of my body and mind
In you, utter fulfillment does find.

Hold on to me, you are my fate
Without you I might death over life debate.

End or No End

Help me to get out of this trap
Away from that dream that was thrown in my lap
These have been some astonishing months
A sensation of rebirth let me take a chance.

Suddenly I experienced being young again
Thrills and lifts I'd thought gone I could attain
Deep into the newly found illusion I buried myself
Put any and all restrictions of age on a shelf.

I knew exactly what I was doing was of no use
But common sense I did vehemently refuse
I fervently hoped to have found
The one on whose flexibility I could count.

Wanted both us to enjoy the make-believe
It did not quite work, instead gave me grief
You, my would-be partner decided not to play
I admit you never did anything encouraging say.

It was me who invented the entire show
You were in ignoring an absolute pro
To lose you I was in constant fear
My own reasoning I decided not to hear.

Sometimes I spend an entire day
Manipulating how to find a way
The foolishness of it I do not want to see
Thus in my imagination you often my lover would be.

To myself I have now to apologize
That I let my body to that point let me drive
Maybe you had an inkling of what I went through
I do not blame you for not knowing what to do.

There are a lot of intriguing traits that I own
So I hope I have at least some entertainment you shown
At this moment I am trying to end it all
Not so sure if I can stick to it or again for you will fall.

It is me who is fully responsible if I get hurt again
And yes I now admit that I cause myself the pain
At this very moment my decision is split
It seems so hard to come back to earth and quit.

Phoenix

Like Phoenix from the ashes
I felt born anew
A kindled spirit touched me
I'm sure you know it's you.

It lit a flame within me
That I never felt before
It totally smothered each cell
Of my deepest, inner core.

Not even an utmost tender caress
Of romance with all its charming finesse
Can match to even the slimmest extent
The vibes of utter delight your messages send.

It is possible that souls here on earth do meet
And an unknown entity combines their beat
It is a very special joy I am feeling
Shell from my mental armor is peeling.

At times as the winged word we undress
Yes or No will diminish the stress
Yet when in public we collaborate
Poetry surely opens the gate.

Are the tears I am crying for real?
Or is a Fata Morgana at spiel?
I feel freed from any daily drudge
Nobody could ever give me that much.

I Believe

She was standing in the parking lot
Cars all around hardly an empty spot
On her face no distress or sign of grief
Rather a stunned expression of disbelief.

Her mind just ran a marathon
Back thirty years since her husband was gone
She begged me over, wanted to be heard
To a fantastic happening she referred.

Her usual quite robust manner now demure
Seemed to say, "I don't know why, but I am sure."
In her hand she held a long, pretty feather
She had just bent down to gather.

Birds in this commercial, busy spot
An expected find they are truly not
She admired the feather and continued to say,
"My husband would've been eighty today."

I was fascinated and held my breath
"Here is what happened when he was close to death
He mentioned that should a feather I find
It is from him, he is here in mind."
I was astonished but believed her every word
Fully convinced a miracle had occurred.

Starry Crust

I sense a crust of odd resistance
Protecting your brain
Which renders any question about
Your actual life in vain.

With your amazing poems you protect
Any inner reality disclosure
They keep you safe and uncommitted
To any exposure.

Have you been hurt so bad?
Do you want to be polite instead of mad?
Does the past forbid you openness to show
My heart, not curiosity, wants to know,

I know that it is not occurring by mistake
From day one I noticed the omissions you make
What is the valid reason at hand?
I promise I'll try to understand.

I yearn to know the man you really are
I refuse to accept you as out-of-reach star.

Tides of Love

I am lost in a sea of emotions
The thoughts are my trustworthy boats
They bounce around on the waves of the waters
Laden with memories of once taken roads.

Surrounded by surges of an insatiable desire
With oceanic force your picture sets afire
While waves of tender sensation
Stimulate a nature-incited elation.

Fervently I try a shore of satisfaction to reach
The sails I set hope my intuition will find the beach
Only two choices this adventure can crown
On the beach let me find you or let me drown.

In the sands of the dunes with you I want to unite
For a while together in love and awaiting the tide.

Under the Umbrella

Under the umbrella, called spell
I came to know you rather well.
When your catching words come my way
Under the umbrella I come to sway.

For quite a while now I tried to figure out
What love, admiration and spells are all about.
I have the powers of a psyche from time to time
Most often when cupid his bells lets chime.

I actually feel the thoughts of people dear to me
Without being told, their deepest concerns I see.
Spells are vibrant declarations of a nameless force
They have in a chosen media their source.

Onto my open umbrella those spells often fall
Slowly one by one to the ground they roll.
I don't want them to get me into their grip
I am afraid that into obsession I might slip.

Then there are the times when my powers I use
My infatuation with you is my excuse!

Vague

I open wide the door for you
So together we can come and decide anew.
Now did you read this but did fully ignore
What this poem is actually written for?

I wanted that double-faced words are born
That at first sight might look like a hint of porn.
But that nothing like that they really do mean
Although as porn they could have been seen.

How could I be so immature?
I had nothing to gain from being demure.
To think of you is a sex elixir
A possessive power I love and fear.

All of this must be the fault of cosmic rays
Which uninvited get into our ways.
You stay polite while I try to tease
It seems to come to you with utter ease.

In my loins intrigue and seduction sing
The sign of a casual, incidental fling.
This is not me, not me at all,
To rules out of space I did victim fall.

The pain of having been fooled,
Makes me leave you alone
I have been over ruled
My heart is chilled to the bone.

Tease

I am so in love but it often does hurt
It is as if vinegar into a smoothie was squirt.
I cannot remember that I ever a love letter wrote
Or during love making into ecstasy did explode.

With you I would love to be naked in bed
Exchanging whims we want to have met
I want to inhale your masculine scent
Imagine how my body yields under your hand.

I know all this can be only be dream
Obsessed with it at times I could scream.
A fine line distinguishes between
Ridicule and tease
Try to understand me, please.

One cannot fabricate a vision
So for now I am left with indecision.
I know I love what I think is you
Yet I'm still wondering what is
Fiction and what is true.

This all started with an innocent play
I am afraid that you still see it this way
As much as I hurt you are not to blame
You have a great talent to monitor this game.

It is your poems that cause me this confusion
That inspire my mind and paint this illusion
Our souls that will meet in the afterlife
To complete for what on earth they did strive

Cherubs

We close the door
We want to be alone
Social entertainment we had before
Now only the two of us are privileged
To Lovers intimate moan.

The sculpture of cherubs on the door
Is a polite "Do not enter"
For you and me now less company is more
We fever in each other's body to center.

Those loving angels on the door
Once touched will ring a bell
Chiming the sound of ecstasy and more
They are the guardian of your and my spell.

WHY

Every sigh wants to be comforted with a pat
But hardly ever a plea is with recognition met
That may tend to turn closeness into resentment
And cause two people life in animosity to spend.

A few kind words could a great difference make
From acknowledgement one would comfort take
But each and every one of us is so self-involved
That begging cries we let in thin air dissolve.

So let's give to each other a bit more attention
After all emphasis is not a new invention.
Or one day it may be us who utter the sigh
And when we get no answer we wonder "WHY."

In Vain

Lead me and take my hand
To the secret foreverland.
The love in my heart belongs to you
My yearning for you is strong and true.

You portray for me an ethereal figure of love
Reality is that you are streetwise and tough.
For me you try to soften your constitution
Myself I fight to let go of too much illusion.

We both try hard as we do care for each other
Yet in the end we no longer can bother.
It is sad but it is clear
Time has come to part with a goodbye and good cheer.

Just Utopia

This time I take your poem to be personal
For the "Hello" yes "Hello" I let myself fall.
If I do not admit this, I will have no peace,
If I do tell the truth, then there will be release.
Now let me see how I can say it best
So that my active mind can get some rest.

We don't know what after death to expect.
Can the meeting of souls really become a fact?
I believe you mean what in your poem you say.
 "Hello" yes "Hello" will show us the way.
If for us only a short time is left on earth
As pre-designated, we better rehearse.

There is no guesswork, no further debating.
We know that a bond, truly sublime, is waiting.
"Hello" yes "Hello" we come to share in a starlit place
 Where souls do join, all equal in beliefs or race.
The confirmation was given to me already on earth
When with your "Hello" yes "Hello" you gave it birth.

The Search

What is wrong and what is right?
I will not and plan not to decide.
Fulfillment of secret desires
is apt to ignite new internal fires.

Time on earth cannot be bought.
Closeness occupies my thought.
Give me a sign of a similar urge.
For both of us it could end the search.

Mine is a strange, deep-rooted want.
With another being I need to bond.
I am therefore ready to explore
facts about vibes, souls and more.

Only recently it has occurred to me
that there might truth in all that be.
The supernatural used to leave me cold.
Why do I wonder now, as I get old?

A desire for a sensual attachment
Let's me explore without resentment.
Any way that a "May be" does show
will a new belief and acceptance grow.

What is You

I love you and do not plan to leave you
Every day, yes, every moment
You surprise me with something new.

Apart from the excitement I feel
When I watch you explode within personal appeal
With every day you disclose a new trait
To see and feel all your changes I can hardly wait.

Yes sometimes I step on you
But I watch that from it no harm you grew
You spoil me with flowers, wild and neat
Leave in the air your musky scent so bitter sweet.

Together in the moonshine we praise our maker
Also for the sunshine we both are takers.
You exhilarate all of my dormant senses
With you I bare myself of all defenses.

Never do we have a fight
Between the two of us all things are right
I tend to you, make all of you grow
YOU my cherished garden, I love you so.

Out of Control

Again you made me forget my gripes
Again I succumb to the spell of your vibes
Again my own mind I cannot control
Again you have occupied my soul.

As I thought I had given up on me and you
As I believed to see what is really true
As I was sadly accepting the bitter end
As for strength I prayers to heaven sent.

Then I heard from you again
Then I knew my efforts to resist are in vain
Then I understood a subliminal force had conquered me
Then it became clear that you will my downfall and lover be.

Call a Spade a Spade

Only lately have I come to see
That you are not THE you, nor am I me.
I now decided to call a spade a spade
Unwilling for the "may be" any longer to wait.

I want your love, your answer I fear
I want to know now, so let me hear.
No longer do I care to linger in doubt
Not to worry, on my friendship you can count.

It seems that with what I think, I contradict.
Love, in-love and lust with each other conflict.
Of course I could stop writing about love
But to suppress my feelings is just too tough.
You are special and skilled in romance
With you at play I had hoped for a chance.